Lincoln
Ports and Wharves

G000123181

on old picture postcards

Mike Taylor

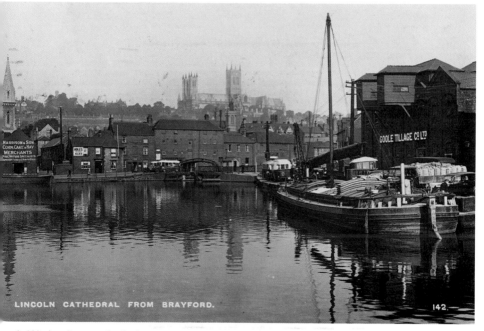

LINCOLN CATHEDRAL FROM BRAYFORD. 142.

1. We begin our clockwise tour around the county with a more modern (1938) view of **Lincoln's** Brayford than that on the front cover. The traditionally busy east wharves have only one vessel moored alongside, allowing the swing road bridge and keeper's hut to be seen clearly. The River Witham flows in from behind the photographer and leaves for Boston beneath this bridge.

ISBN 1 900138 11 5

£3.50

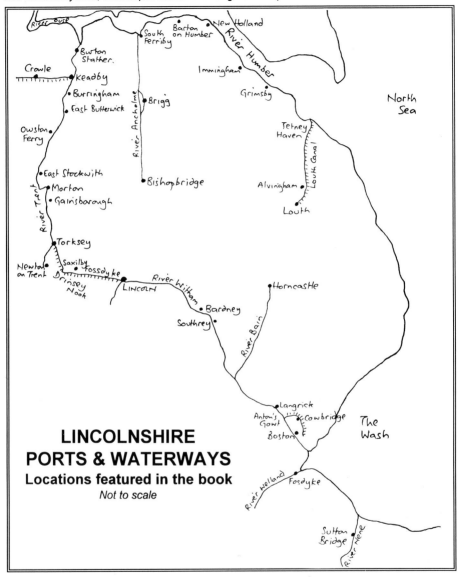

LINCOLNSHIRE
PORTS & WATERWAYS
Locations featured in the book
Not to scale

Designed and Published by
Reflections of a Bygone Age,
Keyworth, Nottingham
1996

Produced and Printed by
Print Rite, School Lane,
Stadhampton, Oxford

2. The Fossdyke, reputedly built by the Romans in AD 120, forms an 11 mile long link between Lincoln and the River Trent. A keel with mast and sail raised, after lowering both to pass beneath **Saxilby's** rail bridge, prepares to resume its voyage to Lincoln. The road swing bridge shown was replaced by a higher fixed bridge in the 1930s. W.Dennis, the village chemist, took this photograph and published the card which was postally used during 1915.

3. Another Dennis production, also featuring a Lincoln-bound sailing keel, taken at the Fossdyke's sharpest bend (a 90° turn at **Drinsey Nook**). It was common practice to clear a ship at Hull, to load craft deeper than the Fossdyke's guaranteed draught and off-load the excess into a lighter kept at Torksey for just such a purpose. The trailing rope indicates that this is the situation here.

Introduction

Much of pre-1974 Lincolnshire (i.e. before Humberside) may be regarded as an island, such that a hypothetical cargo passing down the River Ouse bound from Goole to Boston could travel either via the Humber, North Sea and Wash, or via the River Trent, Fossdyke and River Witham. This booklet chooses to begin at Lincoln and work clockwise around Lincolnshire 'island' with one or two detours.

In a county containing so much flat land and therefore numerous dykes and drains, 'waterways' in this publication have been restricted to rivers or canals that are or have been navigable for cargo-carrying vessels. In addition to the Humber keels and sloops used to carry these cargoes, ferries, both large and small, are well featured together with bridges that succeeded them.

In the thirteenth century, Boston was second only to London in England's list of busiest ports. Grimsby and Gainsborough have seen ships for centuries and these long-established ports have been joined in comparatively recent times by Immingham. Grimsby's fish docks were built and developed to support an age-old tradition of the borough. However, whereas trade at the seaports continues to this day, that to the inland waterway ports, such as Brigg, Gainsborough, Keadby, Lincoln and Louth, has vanished, to be remembered mainly by images on postcards such as those used in this book.

Cards from a wide variety of publishers, many of whom seem to desire anonymity, have been used and credited where this is possible. Lincolnshire supported several excellent localised photographers who produced postcards of their work and selections from the Dennis Series (Saxilby and Torksey), E.W.Carter (Gainsborough and Keadby) and Peakome (Boston) have been included alongside the products of larger local companies such as E.L.Scrivens of Doncaster and Jackson and Son of Grimsby and Bradford. The national publishers Valentine and Raphael Tuck & Sons are also well represented.

Mike Taylor
September 1996

Acknowledgements

I am indebted to Eric Croft of Lincoln for allowing me unrestricted access to his comprehensive collection of postcards of Lincolnshire. The following cards are his: 12-16,22,24,27,32,34,36,43 and 50-53. Also to Geoff Thomas, who kindly allowed me to use two cards (17 and 19) from his albums.

Front cover:
Lincoln's Brayford, once the hub of commercial life in the city, where local produce, together with cargoes from overseas imported via Hull or Boston were discharged from inland waterway craft. Featured on a postally unused E.W.Carter card, with the Cathedral forming an impressive background, this is undoubtedly the most popular viewpoint on the county's waterways.

Back cover (top):
One of the best of many published views of the Trent's Aegre or Aegir, taken by E.W.Carter from the Nottinghamshire bank looking across the river to the ruins of the mill just below **Gainsborough** on which George Elliot's *'Mill on the Floss'* was based. The breaking wave rushes upriver whenever a big incoming tide meets the river's flow.

Back cover (bottom):
A Raphael Tuck and Sons 'Oilette' card, posted at Spalding during 1905, featuring the tidal River Witham at **Boston** looking upstream towards the landmark of St Botolph's church (the stump). Before its docks were constructed in the late nineteenth century, these town centre wharves constituted one of England's biggest ports. John Rennie's cast iron single span Town Bridge built in 1807 is also visible. This was replaced in 1913.

Melton's Village Series. LOCK and BRIDGE, TORKSEY.

4. The Fossdyke's only lock is at **Torksey**, allowing craft to pass to and from the River Trent. The sender of this Melton's Village Series card, posted at Retford in 1905, had a *'splendid trip yesterday on the Trent'*. The lock has double pairs of gates at the lower end; one pair is closed, showing that the river level is below that in the canal. Occasionally, the tidal Trent rises above the Fossdyke and then the other pair of gates (with prominent balance beams) facing the opposite direction is used.

On the Trent, Torksey. no. 4.6.

5. Taken from the Gainsborough-Lincoln road bridge shown on the previous card, this wrongly titled photograph on a postally unused Dennis Series production actually shows craft in **Torksey** Cut between the River Trent (flowing from left to right in the background) and the lock. The keels are waiting for the flood tide to provide sufficient depth of water for them to reach the lock and continue their voyages to Lincoln.

6. Making a detour upriver, the toll bridge built in 1832 between Dunham and **Newton-on-Trent** is encountered. The Trent Navigation Company's paddle tug *Robin Hood* worked daily, towing craft from Torksey to Newark in the 1900s and is seen here on this anonymously produced, postally unused card heading upriver with vessels in tow. *Little John*, well featured in Brian Lund's *'River Trent' (No10 in Yesterday's Nottinghamshire series)* took over at Newark for the voyage to Nottingham.

7. The toll bridge in the background at **Newton-on-Trent** is overshadowed by a newer structure on this unattributed postcard. Following a typhoid outbreak in Lincoln during 1905, bore holes were sunk at Elkesley, near Worksop, to provide a supply of clean water. The pipe bridge shown carries this supply over the river. The system began operation in October 1911 and continues to this day.

28699-J.V.   *TRENT BRIDGE, GAINSBOROUGH. (9)*

8. Ferries were the only means of crossing the Trent in Lincolnshire until **Gainsborough** Bridge was completed in 1791 (Newark had the lowest road crossing of the river until this time). The view on this postally unused Valentine's 'Real Photograph' card was taken looking upstream from the Nottinghamshire bank with the towpath, available for the few horse-hauled craft using the river, visible in the foreground.

W.A.R.Co. 38-18. RIVER TRENT, GAINSBOROUGH.

9. Hull's T.Gray and Company (later United Towing Company), offered a tug service for unpowered craft using the Trent. On this postally unused W.A.R.Co. card, one of the company's steam tugs heads upriver through **Gainsborough** with vessels bound for perhaps Lincoln, Newark and Nottingham in tow.

The Ægir, Gainsborough

10. The Trent negotiates an acute bend at **Morton** below Gainsborough, forming a notorious hazard to river traffic. George Elliot stayed here in 1859 whilst writing *'Mill on the Floss'*, calling it Tofton in the book. An aegre adds interest to the downriver view on this postally unused Valentine's card.

11. Humber keels lie moored close to the Nottinghamshire bank, waiting to lock into West Stockwith basin at one end of the Chesterfield Canal on this postally unused, anonymously published card. Downstream and across the river lies **East Stockwith**, with the two villages linked by the ferry visible in midstream.

12. **Owston Ferry** was a small inland waterway port and this anonymously produced card posted at Haxey in 1922 shows a part-laden keel lying against the wharf during an abnormally high tide. The crane is not in use and a plank from the vessel to the wharf indicates the method of loading/discharge, though the barrow is not visible. Coal for this and nearby villages was brought by water and unloaded in this manner.

13. With over half the picture surface covered by featureless water, the strangely-composed view on this card looking across the Trent shows a small sailing regatta taking place above the ferry landing at **East Butterwick** about 1908. Flood protection work undertaken in the latter half of this century has seen the river banks below Gainsborough raised considerably, changing this and other waterside views.

138-6. Owston Ferry on Regatta Day.

14. With both Trent banks now in Lincolnshire, this Scivens card dating from about 1920, features a view of **Owston Ferry**, on the left bank, from East Ferry. The annual regatta is in progress and a few privileged spectators have been able to use the Humber keel *Doris*, moored in mid-river, as a vantage point.

15. Posted in the village during 1905, this postcard shows the **Burringham** ferryboat preparing to cross to Althorpe at low water with several young villagers as well as reserve boats in view. Some idea of the Trent's tidal range in this stretch may be gained from the high water landing stage visible in the foreground. The M180 motorway river crossing now lies close to this point.

16. Below Burringham, **Keadby** Bridge was completed in 1866 as a rail-only crossing of the Trent, despite objections from Gainsborough merchants, who feared that it would adversely affect the navigation channel up to their town. The view is taken looking downriver. The swing bridge pivoted on the largest of the mid-river piers.

17. Opened in 1916, this Scherzer lift bridge for both road and rail traffic was built at **Keadby**, 66 yards downstream of the previous bridge, and necessitated demolition of Barber's mill visible on the view above. This Scrivens production, posted at Scunthorpe in April 1925 and taken from almost the same viewpoint, is the last in a series of four cards showing the 'King George V Bridge' being raised to allow a sailing keel to pass downriver. The structure still exists, though it ceased to lift in the 1950s.

18. The busy Stainforth and Keadby Canal, part of the Sheffield and South Yorkshire Navigation, had its junction with the Trent at **Keadby**. This postally unused E.W.Carter view is taken looking up the canal from close to the entrance lock which has doubled pairs of gates like the one at Torksey. *Brasso* and *Rupert C* have loaded coal for Hull from the rail-fed coal drops visible on the right hand bank. The horse-drawn tanker *Jim* has just arrived to load another cargo of petrol for Sheffield.

19. In this view from **Crowle's** Great Central Railway station on an E.L.Scrivens card, posted November 1940, a sailing keel is approaching, having been accompanied by the railway all the way from Keadby. The vessel will shortly pass into Yorkshire *(more details of the Sheffield and South Yorkshire Navigation may be found in 'The River Don', No.3 in the 'Yesterday's Yorkshire' Series).*

20. Back on the Trent at **Keadby** jetty below the canal entrance (indicated by the wooden staging in the foreground), two London registered sea-going vessels are loading Yorkshire coal from railway wagons. A postally unused card by Raphael Tuck and Sons Ltd.

21. An E.W.Carter view looking east towards Scunthorpe as a United Towing Company tug begins to turn its tow off Keadby. The three unladen spritsail barges will have come to load Yorkshire coal for London or East Coast ports whilst the laden keel visible will probably be bound for Sheffield via the canal.

LANDING STAGE BURTON STATHER.

22. Many ferry voyages down to Hull and up to Gainsborough were made from the landing stage adjacent to the 'Ferry House Inn' at **Burton Stather**, shown on this E.W. Carter card posted in the nearby village during 1924. The ship *Energie* lies beyond at a cargo wharf that has been extended over the past decades, and now stores large amounts of imported timber.

23. Inland waterway craft are heading down the Trent, seen from one of the few areas of high ground in Lincolnshire at **Burton Hills**. The river is about a mile from its confluence with the Ouse to form the Humber and despite the caption on this postally unused Valentine's Real Photograph card, these latter two rivers are barely visible.

24. Another diversion from our circular path on this c.1920 card shows the warehouses at **Bishopbridge**, the head of the River Ancholme Navigation. A small keel has just discharged its cargo to a cart using the hand crane adjacent to the warehouse. Fertilisers and cattle cake were the major imports here, but the small port was seeing little waterway traffic by the outbreak of World War II.

The Oil Mills, Brigg

25. A new and straighter course for the Ancholme through **Brigg** was cut in the seventeenth century and the Yarborough Oil Mills shown here, as well as a sugar factory, were developed alongside this channel. During the twentieth century, seeds for crushing imported via Hull were brought to the mills by inland waterway craft, some of which may be seen at various stages in the unloading of their cargoes. This traffic ceased in the early 1970s, leaving pleasure craft to have almost exclusive use of the river.

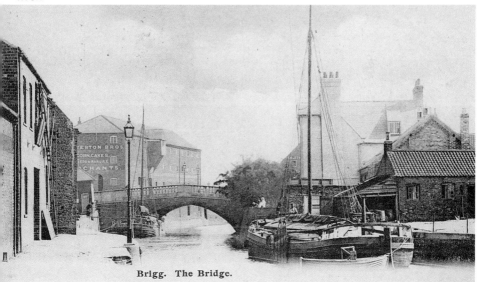

Brigg. The Bridge.

26. The old course of the River Ancholme through **Brigg** is featured on this card, posted in 1903. Referred to as the Coal Dyke because fuel for the gasworks was discharged near here, the stretch of water held a boatyard as well as several general cargo wharves. The upstream view also shows the road bridge, completed in 1828.

27. The Ancholme flowed out into the Humber at **South Ferriby**, and this unattributed card, posted in the village during 1910, features, from left to right, the new sluices fitted in 1903 with a road bridge over them, the navigation lock and the 'Sloop Inn'. The sluices were opened in times of flood whenever the Ancholme level was higher than the tidal Humber, thereby draining much valuable farmland. The view is taken looking north towards the Humber.

28. Below the lock at **South Ferriby** lay this floating dry dock used for repairing wooden craft. Vessels were admitted at high water with the dock on the river bed, and supported as the tide ebbed away. The Humber end was then sealed and the whole assembly floated on the next tide, allowing work to be done on the occupant of the dry dock.

Waterside Road, Barton-on-Humber.

Harrison, photo, Lincoln.

29. A photograph by Harrison of Lincoln featuring Waterside Road, **Barton-on-Humber**, is reproduced on this card published in the Jay Em Jay series by Jackson of Grimsby, and posted at Barton in October 1905. The view is taken looking north as a keel lies moored in the narrow watercourse. Coal was discharged at the small wharf in the foreground.

THE HAVEN BARTON ON HUMBER. 14.

30. Close to the mouth of the creek at **Barton-on-Humber** there were water-served maltings (right) and a boatyard (left) where wooden keels and sloops were built and repaired. A small cog boat is receiving attention to the left of this Humber-facing view.

Ferry Boat, New Holland Pier.

Parker's
RealPhoto Series
New Holland.

31. The **New Holland** ferry across the Humber to Hull was used by many residents of North Lincolnshire before the Humber Bridge was opened in 1981. Here, on this Parker's Real Photo card, published locally and posted in the village during 1915, the coal-fired paddle steamer *Brocklesby* (1912-1935) lies at the pier. This pier was developed in the 1980s for handling coasters carrying bulk cargoes.

THE DOCK, NEW HOLLAND.

32. Another locally produced card, this one by Stevens, also posted in New Holland during 1915, shows **New Holland** dock, which lay just east of the shore end of the ferry pier. A paddle steamer, tug and several inland waterway craft may be seen.

33. At the turn of the century, a new dock was planned for Grimsby. On the Dock Engineer's advice, it was decided to build it closer to the Humber's deep water channel a few miles upriver at **Immingham**. The first sod was cut in 1906 and this artist's impression of an aerial view from above the Humber is featured in a postally unused card published by Jackson and Son of Grimsby in their Jay Em Jay Series.

34. A Shaw of Grimsby card posted in the borough on 25th June 1910, eight days after the event. The Great Central Railway's *S.S. Dewsbury* is seen leaving the western coaling jetty at **Immingham** on its maiden voyage to Antwerp at a time when the dock was under construction. Ships too large to enter the dock were (and still are) handled at this jetty, and at those subsequently built out into the Humber close to this point.

Opening Immingham Dock, July 22nd 1912. S.S. Killingholme entering Kings Dock. 4.

F.C.C. Series.

35. **Immingham Docks** were opened in 1912 by King George V and Queen Mary, who travelled from Grimsby on the paddle steamer *Killingholme*, a Humber ferry and sister ship to the *Brocklesby (see plate 31)*. This postally unused card is one in the F.C.C. Series published at the time. Some of the 1,418 invited guests treated to lunch after the ceremony can be seen on the quayside. The name 'King's Dock' never stuck, 'Immingham Docks' being preferred.

36. Published by R.Freeman of Grimsby and Immingham, this card features one of the first trams to be used on the Grimsby and Immingham Electric Railway, opened in 1912. Built and operated by the Great Central Railway to carry dockers to the new port of **Immingham**, the lines were very busy at times of shift change. The system closed in 1961.

37. Grimsby's Riverhead was formerly part of the havens (harbours) which existed here before the present docks were built. The picture on this card, taken from Victoria Street early this century, shows the steam barge *Quencast* (left) lying at Riverhead after transferring sacks of flour loaded at Hull to carts. A loaded keel lies in mid-river with a plank ashore for discharge of bags of cement brought from Melton on the north bank of the Humber.

38. Steamers and sailing ships are visible in **Grimsby's** Royal Dock on this Jay Em Jay Series card, postally used in 1919. The dock was opened in 1852 by Queen Victoria and had been built to project out into the Humber from Alexandra Dock, the first to be built, in 1800. The Royal Dock is currently the port's principal commercial dock. The 300 foot high dock tower, built in 1854, held 30,000 gallons of water that was originally used for opening lock gates and powering machinery around the dock estate.

39. A short distance downriver from the Royal Dock entrance lie **Grimsby's** fish docks. A steam trawler registered in the borough is leaving one of the dock entrance locks bound for the North Sea fishing grounds. A lifeboat station (left) can also be seen on this W.H.Smith 'Kingsway Real Photo Series' card from c.1910.

AEROFILMS SERIES   GRIMSBY.   FISH DOCK AND TOWER, FROM THE AIR   No. 12666

40. This Aerofilms Series card shows only part of **Grimsby's** fish docks and dates from the 1930s, when this was the country's premier fishing port, supporting a fleet numbered in hundreds. The dock tower and Royal Dock are visible in the background.

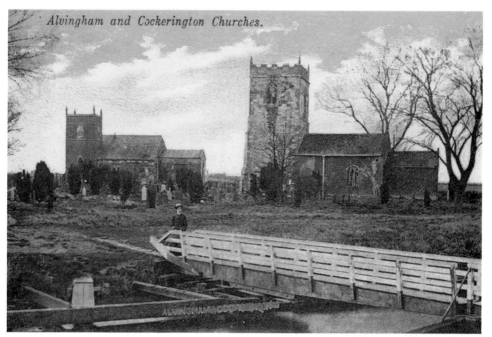

Alvingham and Cockerington Churches.

41. A swing footbridge across the Louth Canal at **Alvingham** is shown on this postally unused card by Clarke and Son of Louth. The rare sight of two churches (Alvingham and Cockerington) sharing a common churchyard may be seen in the background.

Tetney Lock, near Cleethorpes

42. The 12-mile, 8-lock Louth Canal, completed in 1770, met tidal waters at **Tetney** Haven. This card, showing the canal's entrance lock, again with two pairs of lower gates visible, was posted at Birdness in August 1909.

34   The Louth Disaster, Ma...
Jam of Barges at Riv...

1920.
d.

W. Benton
82 Rye Hill
Newcastle on Tyne.

43. Commemorating the flash flood at **Louth** in May 1920, this is card No 34 and the last in the series published by W.Benton of Newcastle-on-Tyne. 23 people were killed as a result of the rainstorm and these barges were torn from their moorings on the River Lud and flung against the first lock of the Louth Canal. The disaster effectively closed the waterway permanently.

1207 Swing Bridge, Sutton Bridge

44. Before heading up the Witham, two Lincolnshire sites on other rivers which feed into the Wash merit mention. The River Nene, giving access to Wisbech and Peterborough for sea-going craft, was first bridged at **Sutton Bridge** in 1831. In the 1860s, a rail track was added but damage caused by trains necessitated construction of a new bridge 100 yards upstream with separate road and rail crossings. Opened in 1897, it is seen here swung open to allow *Prima* to pass downstream. The bridge was converted to two-way road traffic in 1960 as the railway closed.

Fosdyke Bridge. 1915.

45. The River Welland also allowed shipping from the Wash to travel further inland and reach Spalding. At **Fosdyke**, once a bathing resort, a bridge was erected in 1815, to carry the Boston-King's Lynn road. The iron swing bridge shown at low water on this unattributed card, bearing jotted notes on the village's history, was completed as a replacement in 1911.

The Dock, Boston

46. Heading up the River Witham from the Wash, **Boston's** enclosed Dock is encountered after 4½ miles. Opened in 1884 with an entrance lock visible in the background, the small dock remains busy to this day. The fish docks lay to the right of this view and, as the card posted in 1922 shows, timber was one of its major imports. It still is, along with steel and paper.

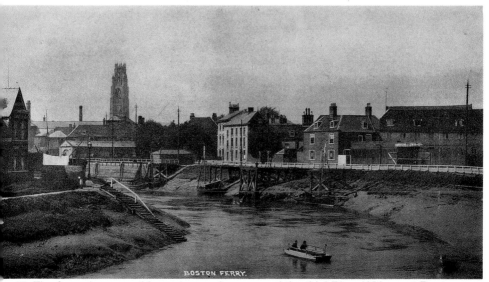

BOSTON FERRY.

47. The ferry shown on this upstream view crossed the tidal River Witham at **Boston** between Pulvertoft Lane (left) and Skirbeck Road. The wooden jetties shown were replaced by a vertical wall early this century, making access to the ferry difficult, especially at low water, and the service was discontinued. Haven Bridge, built in 1964, now crosses the river here. Postcard published by Frith of Reigate.

A Match at Cowbridge, Boston.

48. This card by Peakome of Boston, posted from there to Sheffield in 1907, shows a fishing match in progress on the Maud Foster Drain which John Rennie widened in the early 1800s as part of his Fenland drainage scheme. The view is taken looking south past the **Cowbridge** House Inn on this part of the Witham Navigable Drains, still popular with anglers today.

49. **Boston's** Grand Sluice was built in 1760 as part of a fen drainage scheme, and maintained a navigable depth upstream on the River Witham. It is shown on this Valentine's series card No. 54779. The lock situated just beyond the left-hand bridge arch was too short for most inland waterway craft, and they had to wait until water levels above and below the lock had equated before passing through. The rail bridge was built in 1885 to replace the original 1846 structure.

50. Entry to the Witham Navigable Drains from the River Witham is through the lock at **Anton's Gowt**, shown on this card published by E.W.Peakome of Boston. The view, almost unchanged today, was taken looking across the river. the 'Oak Tree Inn' and Restaurant is visible beyond the lock.

51. Until 1907, when a bridge was completed to the right of this view, a ferry was used to cross the Witham at **Langrick**. This card, also published by Peakome, shows the flat-decked chain ferry, as well as two pleasure craft and a smaller passenger ferry on the west bank of the river.

52. The River Bain, on which the Horncastle and Tattershall Canal had been based, was defunct as a navigable waterway before 1890. The wharfside in **Horncastle**, to which craft used to trade, is visible on this Jay Em Jay Series card, again featuring a photograph by Harrison of Lincoln.

53. This anonymously published card was posted in July 1908 and shows the **Southrey** chain ferry being wound across the Witham watched by villagers situated near the double track railway which linked Lincoln with Boston until 1970.

The Sugar Beet Factory from Bridge, Bardney

54. Bardney's sugar beet factory, seen here from the Witham's right bank, was built in 1927 and originally received some of its raw material by water. Nowadays everything comes by road to a much enlarged factory which occupies the site and works 24 hours a day, 7 days a week, for a 4-5 month period each year.

Bardney Bridge

55. Swinging round from this view on the card above to face upriver, a Humber keel and narrowboat are moored beyond **Bardney** Bridge built about 1910 to carry the Lincoln road and replace a ferry. A water tower shows the position of the railway, built in 1848 along the Witham bank, which was mainly responsible for the demise of waterway traffic on the river.